DI032822

Patrick Kavanagh

THE IRISH WRITERS SERIES
James F. Carens, General Editor

BRIAN MOORE	Jeanne Flood
PATRICK KAVANAGH	Darcy O'Brien
OLIVER ST. JOHN GOGARTY	J. B. Lyons
GEORGE FITZMAURICE	Arthur E. McGuinness
GEORGE RUSSELL (AE)	Richard M. Kain and James H. O'Brien
IRIS MURDOCH	Donna Gerstenberger
MARY LAVIN	Zack Bowen
FRANK O'CONNOR	James H. Matthews
ELIZABETH BOWEN	Edwin J. Kenney, Jr.
WILLIAM ALLINGHAM	Alan Warner
SEAMUS HEANEY	Robert Buttel
THOMAS DAVIS	Eileen Sullivan

PATRICK KAVANAGH

Darcy O'Brien

Lewisburg
BUCKNELL UNIVERSITY PRESS
London: ASSOCIATED UNIVERSITY PRESSES

821.91
KAV

Associated University Presses, Inc.
Cranbury, New Jersey 08512

Associated University Presses
108 New Bond Street
London W1Y OQX, England

Library of Congress Cataloging in Publication Data

O'Brien, Darcy.
  Patrick Kavanagh.

  (The Irish writers series)
  Bibliography: p.
  1. Kavanagh, Patrick, 1904–1967.
PR6021.A74Z84   821'.9'12   73–168818
ISBN 0–8387–7884–4
ISBN 0–8387–7985–9 pbk.

Printed in the United States of America

16,863

Contents

Chronology

1904 Born October 21, at Inniskeen, County Monaghan.

1916 Leaves school, begins writing poetry.

1928– First verses published in *Weekly Independent*
29 and *Dundalk Democrat*; AE (George Russell) accepts verses for his *Irish Statesman.*

1930 Makes pilgrimage to Dublin on foot.

1936 First book published, *The Ploughman and Other Poems.*

1938 *The Green Fool* (autobiographical novel) appears and is withdrawn after libel suit by Oliver St. John Gogarty.

1939 Moves to Dublin.

1942 *The Great Hunger* published.

1947 *A Soul for Sale* (poems) published.

1948 *Tarry Flynn* (novel) published.

1952 April to May; edits, writes and publishes with the help of his brother, Peter, *Kavanagh's Weekly,* a journal of literature and politics.

1954 Libel trial, Kavanagh v. *The Leader.*

1955 Cancerous lung removed; receives stipend for life from University College, Dublin, through intervention of the Taoiseach (Prime Minister) John A. Costello.

1958   *Recent Poems* published by the Peter Kavanagh Hand Press.
1960   *Come Dance with Kitty Stobling* (poems) published.
1963   Broadcasts *Self-Portrait* (published as a book the next year) over Irish Television.
1964   *Collected Poems* published.
1965   Travels to America to lecture at Northwestern University; by this time he spends several weeks each year in London.
1967   Marries Katharine Moloney in Dublin; his *Collected Pruse* published; dies November 30.

I

The Great Hunger

Much can be learned from the poetry and prose of Patrick Kavanagh: details and patterns of Irish country life, the atmosphere of literary Dublin, the revelations and frustrations of a single soul. Yet a good poet, aged about forty at the present writing, has stated that Patrick Kavanagh did truly liberate him and his generation "but he liberated us into ignorance." Kavanagh limited himself, it is true, to writing about himself only and the ways of life that formed him, although he extended his range somewhat in his journalism. But after Yeats and Joyce, immediately after them, perhaps self-limitation was the best course for an Irish writer, since the history of the human race, the nature of the unseen world, the possibilities of linguistic experiment, and what Kavanagh liked to call contemptuously "the Irish thing" all had been adequately covered. What was left? Daily life. Mud, stones, flowers, food, drink, faces, joy, sickness, hope, despair, spite, resentment, family, love, hate, and the occasional intimation of—something. No symbols anywhere. In "Is" (1958) Kavanagh wrote: "The only true teaching/Subsists in watching/Things moving or just colour/Without comment from the scholar." Kavanagh knew that it was difficult for a poet to get by without adopting some symbol or theory as his own: Yeats's masks and gyres. But he could not honestly find anything appropriate unless, as he once said half-facetiously, it was the magpie.

There are allusions aplenty, even the odd conundrum here and there in Kavanagh, but their context is the clay of Monaghan and the streets of Dublin, not a literary copybook. Kavanagh tried to be parochial without being provincial, he wrote of the universal particular. "Parochialism and provincialism," Kavanagh used to say, "are direct opposites. A provincial is always trying to live by other people's loves, but a parochial is self-sufficient." Most Irish writing of this century, whatever its quality, has been aimed at foreign markets, produced as an exportable commodity, like beef or family crests. Irish writers, living in a colonial or post-colonial situation, have like their counterparts in other emerging nations tried to prove to themselves that they are human by gaining the respect and attention of their former colonial masters, even when their fear of inferiority is masked by patriotic rhetoric and reference, or when they appear to care little one way or the other about the colonizers. Much of Joyce's energy came from his desire to make himself lord of the English language, master, as it were, in the master's house. He did, and in so doing he left little in that way for his Irish successors to prove. Eventually they would turn to the examination of their own ways of life and not care so much who was looking.

At worst this sort of post-colonial egoism makes for complacency and empty, defensive pride, as it did for the Irish Free State after 1927, with its censorship laws, designed as if to prove that Ireland had nothing to learn from the rest of the world. There is a touch of such complacency in Kavanagh and in the course of this study I shall have occasion to wonder whether he did not limit his verse and the range of his mind too severely. But the weight of his writing falls against those of his countrymen who boasted of their insular Irishness, taking as their self-definition fantasies about Celtic blood, cultivating traits and poses designed, Kavanagh would say, by foreigners or by Irish writers desirous of pleasing foreigners. "I do not believe," wrote Kavanagh, "that there is any such thing as 'Irish' in literature." Joyce had said the same thing by making the hero of his Dublin epic a Jew.

Kavanagh's attitude to nationalism in literature was extreme and, as we shall have reason to note, at times inconsistent. But he was part of a general literary reaction against mythopoeic notions of Irishness, a reaction given new impetus today by the bloodshed supposedly sanctified by ghosts and myths in Northern Ireland, myths and ghosts both Catholic and Protestant. One of the greatest of modern short stories, "Guests of the Nation," by Frank O'Connor, first published in 1931, marks the beginnings of attempts in Irish writing to cast off the old nationalist distinctions and fantasies, though obviously they persist. The story grew out of O'Connor's disillusion with politics (he fought on the Republican side during the Civil War), and it tells of how two Englishmen are shot to death in cold blood for the sake of the Republican cause. In the course of the story we have come to know the two Englishmen and their captors as individual men. As the narrator says, "And anything that happened to me afterwards, I never felt the same about again." The common humanity of men and the willingness of fanatics to ignore that commonality for the sake of some abstraction are what alter the narrator's consciousness, as they did O'Connor's. Kavanagh loved ridiculing nationalist abstractions, and he had never been caught up in them, except as a youthful diversion. He was too aware of the hungers of daily existence for patriotism to do anything for his physical or spiritual digestion.

When he came to Dublin in the late 'thirties he made certain people uncomfortable, as they in turn made him. The Literary Renaissance was petering out, but many were still anxious to be peasants and to play the Gael. Kavanagh was the real thing, or rather, his existence mocked mendacious, sentimental images of the true Ireland as manufactured by people with smooth hands and voices. He stood five feet ten and a half inches, weighed about a hundred and ninety pounds, had big bones, an eleven foot, great roots of hands; in his youth he carried easily sacks of barley weighing two hundred and fifty pounds. His public style in Dublin was blunt, gruff, rough-hewn and frequently abusive. "I've read your book and it's no good," he would greet a fellow-writer in a voice like coal sliding down a chute. Or, "I've not read your book but I know it's no good," the friendlier greeting. Like any countryman, he allowed himself little outward display of sentiment or enthusiasm, though his verse sheltered plenty of both, and on Pembroke Road you could see him

> Dishevelled with shoes untied,
> Playing through the railings with little children
> Whose children have long since died.
> O he was a nice man,

Fol dol the di do,
He was a nice man
I tell you.
("If Ever You Go To Dublin Town")

Often he was goaded by journalists and third-rate literary types into a degree of vituperativeness that was almost self-parodying, but he got in many a good kick before the end, for which he payed the price of being ignored or patronized. He was willing to be disliked, perhaps too willing.

Certain factors then ought to be kept in mind as we move into a discussion of Kavanagh's verse. He was in revolt against fake nationalist sentiment and images, and he was, in his best work, concerned with capturing the poetry of ordinary life as he knew it. He tried to present this life bare, unadorned by received literary conventions or by flashy literary techniques. At the same time he often managed to get into his lines a spiritual quality that lifts them a little above mere matter. The nationalistic emphasis of much of the Literary Renaissance was abhorrent to him, but the spare, direct, personal style of Yeats's later work was an undoubted influence on him, as it has been on all recent Irish poets of any merit. He had no use for Joyce's ballet of rhetoric, styles and symbols, but Joyce the mimic of life was a continuous influence on Kavanagh, who named *Ulysses* as his "second-favourite bedside book." (*Moby Dick* was the first favorite.) He would have agreed with Frank O'Connor that *Ulysses* "is at its greatest not in its construction, which is haphazard, nor in its rhetorical experiments, which are frequently otiose, but in its description of the poetry of everyday life in Dublin in the first decade of

this century. . . . The streets, the shops, the public-
houses recorded forever by a man with an uncanny eye
and a splendid ear are unique in the literature of the
world." Well, not quite, that is too simple; but if O'Connor had added that *Ulysses* is also the history of a soul,
Kavanagh would have agreed.

It must also be understood that Kavanagh's work is
the product of a very low, dispirited period in Irish life
and literature, the sort of psychological slump that most
nations emerging from colonial rule experience after the
revival of the past fails and people become aware that
they have to make do with the rubble left behind by the
departed conqueror. The Anglo-Irish war of independence had been followed by a Civil War, it in turn
followed by years of political strife, and at last the
energies, hopes and ideals of the Revolution had been
exhausted. Forty, thirty, even twenty years before, it had
been possible to be caught by the magic of a national
literature that appeared to have disinterred the past by
way of shaping an exalted vision of the future. By 1940,
when Kavanagh began doing his best work, national
independence was a reality but the vision had blacked
out, and Ireland seemed to the most sensitive of her
writers a dismal hole, its citizens becoming obsessed with
ambitions of bourgeois respectability, isolated from the
world by circumstances and by a perverse self-will. The
neutrality of the nation during World War II, an expression of freedom from British policy and consistent
with the Government's professed commitment to an end
to British rule in the six northeastern counties (Northern
Ireland), made this isolation all the more complete.
Having seen the nationalist myths dissolve, disheartened
by the values of the developing society, the better Irish

writers had by 1940 turned caustically critical. Most got themselves banned. Sean O'Faolain used his editorial columns in *The Bell* to attack the Government and the Church. The most talented novelist of the period, Flann O'Brien, ended one of his novels with a meditation on suicide, another with a purgative gush of vomit; a third is in its entirety a psychic map of hell. Samuel Beckett preferred living in France at war than in Ireland at peace. And Kavanagh's most important single poem, *The Great Hunger* (1942), is an exegesis of the squalor of Irish country life.

In October, 1952, *The Leader*, now defunct but then a well-known Dublin weekly paper, published a "Profile" of Patrick Kavanagh that predicted that he "will be gratefully remembered by the Irish nation for what is probably the best poem written in Ireland since Goldsmith gave us *The Deserted Village. The Great Hunger* and several of his short lyrics are assured of permanence because of the intense personal vision that informs them and because of the verbal genius which gives that vision expression."

Fair enough. But the irony of it is that the rest of this "Profile" was a personal attack on Kavanagh sufficiently vicious to inspire the poet to sue for libel. He asked £10,000 damages, expected to get £500, and got nothing, the jury finding for the defendants.

I shall discuss the trial further on, because it is irresistible. Here note only that even Kavanagh's detractors (Brendan Behan, with whom Kavanagh had a running feud, and Valentine Iremonger, a poet and an official in the Department of External Affairs, are thought to have been the authors of the anonymous "Profile") had to admit his talent. To call *The Great*

Hunger the best poem written in Ireland since *The Deserted Village* one has to pass over quite a lot of Yeats. Perhaps the authors of the "Profile" wished to compromise the few positive things they had to say about Kavanagh by inflating them to the point of incredulity, but *The Great Hunger* is a work of immense and permanent power. Few people outside Ireland have ever heard of it, and this is a pity, for the poem's sake and for the sake of understanding modern Irish literature.

Sections of it were first published in 1942 in Cyril Connolly's *Horizon* magazine. That issue was quickly banned, and two policemen raided Kavanagh's flat in Pembroke Road, one of them holding a copy of the poem behind his back. "Did you write that?" he asked. Kavanagh was courteous to the Vice Squad but of course at the time he saw the raid as persecution of the artist by Philistines. Censorship had become maniacally, absurdly vigorous. Debates on the merits of books fouled the Dail (Parliament) and, during the War, a strict newspaper censorship was imposed as well.

It is difficult to explain the Vice Squad's interest in *The Great Hunger*. One passage implies masturbation and in another the word "arse" appears, but more alarming still, the poem appears to be anti-Irish and therefore could be taken as obscene on its face. At any rate the Cuala Press brought out an edition of 250 copies in 1942, an abridged version was included in *A Soul for Sale* (1947), and the complete version was reprinted in *Collected Poems* (1964) and in the *Complete Poems* (1972). In 756 lines, divided into fourteen sections, the poem describes the life of Patrick Maguire, a small farmer in a place unnamed but resembling in detail Kavanagh's native ground in County Monaghan. It starts rather portentously—"Clay is the word and clay is the flesh/Where the potato-gatherers like mechanised/ scarecrows move . . ." (I, 1–2) and ends theatrically— "The hungry fiend/Screams the apocalypse of clay/In every corner of the land." (XIV, 75–77) But in between the maddening, deadening details of country life, the stunted energies and hopes of people tethered to the land come across in concise images with great emotional impact. *The Great Hunger* has the power of a natural force, a flood or a drought.

I am not sure how to account for this natural force, it is so natural. Its rhythms are mostly those of common speech, often willing itself to rhyme, sounding sometimes vaguely ballad like, but on the whole deliberately flat, dreary, and irregular, with the hint of an Irish air or even a nursery rhyme in the meter.

> Sitting on a wooden gate,
> Sitting on a wooden gate,
> Sitting on a wooden gate
> He didn't care a damn.
> Said whatever came into his head,
> Said whatever came into his head,
> Said whatever came into his head
> And inconsequently sang.
> (VII, 1–184)

Kavanagh wrote the poem in a rush. "One evening in 1941," his brother, Peter, recalls, "when I returned from teaching school Patrick showed me the first two pages of a long verse he had begun. Great stuff I replied excitedly and urged him to continue at once, not to delay a minute until he had it completed. He took me at my word as he always did in such circumstances and in two or three days had completed *The Great Hunger*. It was written in pen of course since neither of us owned a typewriter. Since then he rewrote this verse in pen and sold the 'original' manuscript to numerous collectors.'' The poem made Kavanagh's reputation and later he had the distinction of having the title stolen, or so he thought, by Cecil Woodham-Smith for a best seller about the famine of the 1840s.

But Kavanagh's *Great Hunger* is the spiritual, intellectual, and sexual hunger of the Irish countryman, who whatever else he lacks usually has enough to eat, milk and praties (potatoes), the bacon joint and cabbage in better times, as during world wars, when farm prices go up. The tone of *The Great Hunger* ranges from somber to bitter, to wistful to futile, and it is more bitter than anything else. The glib and riotous peasants of Synge, the droll country wits of Lady Gregory, the hard-riding country gentlemen and romantic beggarmen of Yeats— all are absent. The leaders of the Literary Renaissance had been members of the Protestant Ascendancy. Yeats had written that, "John Synge, I and Augusta Gregory, thought/All that we did, all that we said or sang/Must come from contact with the soil, ... " But their contact with the soil was of a very limited sort. They were agricultural-poetical tourists and in their works they produced an attractive, glamorized version of peasant life that rings false, though beautifully false. Thus Kavanagh:

> The world looks on
> And talks of the peasant:
> The peasant has no worries;
> In his little lyrical fields
> He ploughs and sows;

Patrick Kavanagh

He eats fresh food,
He loves fresh women,
He is his own master
As it was in the Beginning
The simpleness of peasant life.
(XIII, 1–10)

Kavanagh was fond of calling the Literary Renaissance "a thoroughgoing English-bred lie." Certainly his idea of country truth has nothing of the Celtic Twilight about it. His Patrick Maguire is like a rural version of one of Joyce's paralyzed characters in *Dubliners:* "Watch him, watch him, that man on a hill whose spirit/ Is a wet sack flapping about the knees of time." (I, 58–59) He is faithful, but to death. He stays with his mother till she dies at ninety-one, and

When she died
The knuckle-bones were cutting the skin of her son's backside
And he was sixty-five.
O he loved his mother
Above all others.
O he loved his ploughs
And he loved his cows
And his happiest dream
Was to clean his arse
With perennial grass
On the bank of some summer stream;
To smoke his pipe
In a sheltered gripe
In the middle of July—
His face in a mist
And two stones in his fist
And an impotent worm on his thigh.
(II, 6–22)

Evenings there is idle, monosyllabic conversation at the crossroads, a stone thrown, talk of women and horses, the sound of his sister grunting in bed, of "a sow taking up a new position." A cup of cocoa for him, a chunk of wheaten bread, and

> Pat opened his trousers wide over the ashes
> And dreamt himself to lewd sleepiness.
> The clock ticked on. Time passes.
>
> (V, 33–5)

Always he is giving himself another year, to wait for money or marriage, to break out of the circle he walks round his irregular fields twenty times each day. He might see a girl, rush beyond her in his mind, and think sin: "For the strangled impulse there is no redemption." He strokes "the flanks of his cows in lieu of wife to handle." Only the animals breed, as the people rot, boys and girls withering down from day dreams to the grave. Such dreams Maguire has, of health and wealth and love, are, " . . . three stones too sharp to sit on,/Too hard to carve. Three frozen idols of a speechless muse." (VI, 20–1) We glimpse Maguire at last under the ground, hardly remembering life at all:

> If he opens his eyes once in a million years—
> Through a break in the crust of the earth he may see a face nodding in
> Or a woman's legs. Shut them again for that sight is sin.
>
> (XIV, 46–8)

The Great Hunger is tragedy without drama because

Maguire never contests anything, has no energy to struggle. We are aware only of the hunger-ache in him, and it is only that which distinguishes him from the farm animals. The few excerpts above give slight notion of the cumulative force of the poem but they should suggest the direct simplicity of its language and images and the unadorned authenticity of its detail. It is a didactic work. Kavanagh wrote it in a messianic frame of mind. It preaches, sometimes sarcastically, always bitterly, against the dull misery of the life it describes. Maguire, his family, and his neighbors are neither praised nor blamed: they are destroyed by a murder-machine that is green and smells good in the spring. This view of Irish country life was not unique in Irish literature by 1942, but such hardness and bleakness of vision had been concentrated in prose, especially in the short story, and even there a portion of lyric description or speech would usually lighten the atmosphere or ennoble it—or, as Kavanagh would say, falsify it. In the stories of Liam O'Flaherty, for example, we get a sense of the nobility of people in their suffering, and we admire certain characters as much as we are appalled by their fate. At last, Patrick Maguire is not noble. Whatever dream or dignity he had in him the clay has choked. When finally he is underground and "The tongue in his mouth is the root of a yew," we know that he was dead long before he died anyway.

Neither does *The Great Hunger* show any admiration or respect for the rural society of which Maguire is a part. The people of the townland work, play cards, idle, die. Rarely, they breed. And the women are distinguished from the men only in that their tongues are sharper. "O Christ!" Maguire thinks, "I am locked in a stable with pigs and cows for ever."

No crash,
No drama.
That was how his life happened.
No mad hooves galloping in the sky,
But the weak, washy way of true tragedy—
A sick horse nosing around the meadow for a clean place
to die.

(XIII, 54–6)

2

Stony Grey Soil

In later years Kavanagh took to disparaging *The Great Hunger*. There were "some queer and terrible things" in it "but it lacks the nobility and repose of great poetry." It began to seem overdone, overstated. He wondered whether the Vice Squad had been right after all: "There is something wrong with a work of art, some kinetic vulgarity in it when it is visible to policemen. . . . *The Great Hunger* is tragedy and Tragedy is underdeveloped Comedy, not fully born. Had I stuck to the tragic thing in *The Great Hunger* I would have found many powerful friends."

Such remarks are partly the poet's predictable disowning of early work and partly the preference of an older man for grays over the blacks and whites of his youth. But for all its power the poem never did represent with any degree of fullness or completeness Kavanagh's attitudes and feelings about the land. Here is a tired aesthetic problem: "sincerity." Ought we to care a whit whether a poet believes in what he says as long as he says it well? Probably not. But if "sincerity" ought to be no issue for the reader, it can become one for the writer. Kavanagh never mastered Yeats's trick of changing masks comfortably from poem to poem.

I believe that *The Great Hunger* was written as a polemic not so much against the land as against sentimental literary lies about the land. Kavanagh was cynical about the reputations that had been gained by these lies; yet he had still more to be cynical about when his own lie, "the tragic thing in *The Great Hunger*," proved profitable too. He began to notice that his dishonest poems, or poems reflecting one rather than two or seven sides of a subject, attracted the most attention. They helped to sound a steady note of either lamentation or exultation, for the benefit of one-track ears. One of his least favorite poems, "Memory of Brother Michael" (1944), became the most frequently anthologized. ("A nettle-wild grave . . . Ireland's stage. . . .") It has just the right clap-trap, the perfect cliché-touch. The Irish thing.

Kavanagh's poetic problem after *The Great Hunger* was to find a way of getting in some of the things he had excluded without sacrificing all the queer and terrible aspects. His earlier work (1930–39) consisted mainly of pious encomiums: "I find a star-lovely art/In a dark sod./Joy that it timeless! O heart/That knows God!/ ("Ploughman," 1930)" But this was as much a distortion as the apocalypse of clay. We can gather from his two autobiographical novels, *The Green Fool* (1938) and *Tarry Flynn* (1947), and from his letters and fugitive journalism, how varied and complicated Kavanagh's relation to the land actually was.

Benedict Kiely has described *The Green Fool*, accurately, as being "as honest and unaffected and happy and humorous a book as any young poet ever wrote about himself." Yet its publishing history was a disaster. After his first book of verse, *Ploughman and Other Poems,* had come out in 1936, Kavanagh went to London to try to get involved in the literary scene. He quickly ran out of money, tried selling coronation medals in the company of an amputee, and passed himself off to a newspaper as the man who had blown up the statue of George II in Dublin, earning a guinea for his lie. But Helen Waddell, the novelist, was kind to him and suggested that he write an autobiographical novel. Kavanagh returned to Ireland and completed the book in a year.

Shortly after publication *The Green Fool* was withdrawn, and Kavanagh earned neither fame nor a penny from it, though a little notoriety. Oliver St. John Gogarty (Joyce's model for Buck Mulligan in *Ulysses*) took offense, or said he did, at a certain passage, in which Kavanagh tells of arriving in Dublin after a pilgrimage on foot from his home in Inniskeen, County Monaghan. Knocking, uninvited, on Gogarty's door, "I mistook Gogarty's white-robed maid for his wife—or his mistress. I expected every poet to have a spare wife." This is hardly malicious: if it cuts at anything it is at the country boy's gaucherie. But Gogarty sued successfully for £100 damages and killed the book. Later he joked that he had been offended by the implication that he had but one mistress. Later, too, Kavanagh claimed to have invented the entire incident.

It is one of the few instances known in which Gogarty, who had a vicious tongue but was capable of kindness, lived up to the meanness of character Joyce ascribed to him. Obviously the withdrawal of the book seriously affected Kavanagh's career. *The Green Fool* might well have been a success, for it has a mature, easy tone that Kavanagh was not to recapture for many years, and the savagery of *The Great Hunger* must have been born in part out of his literary frustrations. In the course of describing the blossoming of a poetic soul *The Green Fool* touches on countless details of country life that are of anthropological as well as literary interest.

Kavanagh's father, James, a shoemaker by trade, married Bridget Quinn of Tullerain, County Louth, in 1897. They had ten children, Annie, Mary, Bridget, Patrick (born October 21, 1904), Lucy, Theresa, Josie, James (who died in infancy), Cecelia, and Peter (born March 19, 1916). The original family house in Inniskeen, near the Armagh border of County Monaghan was a traditional Irish cabin, wedge-shaped "to trick the western winds," with two rooms and a kitchen, built and first thatched in 1791. But in 1909, when Patrick was about five, it was torn down and a new house, two-storied and slate-roofed, was built on its foundations. Patrick remembered his father's supplying the two masons who built the house with two dozen bottles of porter a day; they built a healthy structure, light, dry, and roomy. Neighbors were of the opinion that the Kavanaghs must have got a legacy to be able to afford it, but the shoemaker Kavanagh worked hard, from six in the morning till near midnight each day. (His workshop was the kitchen, alive with the talk of customers and journeyman cobblers, telling of their travels.) In addition Kavanagh's mother did a small bit of farming with her children's help. There were about four acres of land and two acres of bog attached to the house, and an acre or two more could be rented from a nearby estate. The Kavanaghs kept about six dozen hens, three cows, and four pigs fattening. Whenever they attempted to add a fifth pig, one would die, so they stuck to the four.

Such were the rudiments of the life portrayed in *The*

Great Hunger but Kavanagh's attitude toward them had more of tolerance and affection than bitter resentment in it, and he returned to Inniskeen regularly throughout his life, in thought, verse, and person, oftener as he grew older. The stunted hills with their outcroppings of rock, hills neither grand nor fertile, held his attention. *The Great Hunger* by itself can mislead one into thinking that Kavanagh's was the case of the Irish writer who finds home conditions so intolerable that he must, so he says, like Shaw or Joyce, flee to save himself. He had literary ambitions and he went, eventually, to Dublin to further them, but Inniskeen, ignorant, backward, slow, he understood and loved too well ever to reject, drawing on it all his life in verse. At times, to be sure, he railed against it:

> O stony grey soil of Monaghan
> The laugh from my love you thieved;
> You took the gay child of my passion
>
> And gave me your clod-conceived. . . .
> You sang on steaming dunghills
> A song of cowards' brood,
> You perfumed my clothes with weasel itch,
> You fed me on swinish food.
>   ("Stony Grey Soil," 1940)

Hate can make a poem strong. Kavanagh had been living in Dublin for over a year when he wrote "Stony Grey Soil," and the city makes every countryman hate himself for awhile. But he knew and eventually expressed that Inniskeen was a way of life, like any other, and that only his unsureness about himself had made him hate it: "Ashamed of what I loved/I flung her from me and called her a ditch/Although she was smiling at me with violets . . . ("Innocence," 1950)

In *The Green Fool*, as later in *Tarry Flynn*, the character and the characters of Inniskeen come across as so varied and so intense that one looks on in fascination and with little enough of either approval or disgust. Had Gogarty not got there first, certain people who appear in the book are said to have been threatening libel suits, but then the Irish are a litigious folk. Certainly Kavanagh does not spare himself from humorous treatment, as when he describes how he taunted the son of the Protestant sexton and then ran for his life from the wrath of the boy's father. Everyone seems to get his due, and no more.

There is nothing stage-Irish here, the observations are too precise for that. We get a sharply focused picture of a specific region and proof that there are not one or two but hundreds of Irelands tucked away among low hills or high mountains, black-soiled valleys or white-stoned coasts; a country as yet unhomogenized by the mass media; a place where crossing a stream can bring a change of accent and custom.

Historically County Monaghan is part of the province of Ulster, a name lately debased into a synonymn for Northern Ireland, whereas Ulster embraces the nine northernmost of Ireland's 32 counties, Northern Ireland but six of these. One detects many of the characteristics of the Ulsterman among the Kavanaghs and their neighbors. These are people with razor edges round their personalities. Extravagant speech is rare. Conversations are apt to be blunt though ironical and often witty, with little of the baroque evasiveness characteristic of the south and west. A cow has died and it is buried at night to avoid the public disgrace of the loss of property. But one neighbor-woman sniffs things out:

"Who was that ye had out there?"
"Biddy Magee."
"A bad-minded article."
"She heard the cow died."
"Well, let her hear away. The cow's gone now and all our bad luck be with her!"
"Amen."

Or take this exchange over the death of a generally despised policeman, known for his strict enforcement of the law against herding animals in the road. Constable Kinsella had joined the British Army at the outbreak of the First World War and was killed the first week:

"Kinsella was a bad article," one of our neighbors said.
"A bad pill surely," was the reply.
"It was the price of him," people said, "he couldn't have better luck."

This sort of acid banter embodies the psychology and general outlook of Kavanagh country. Inniskeen lies in a townland (or district) called Mucker, meaning in corrupted Irish-Gaelic a place where pigs breed in abundance, and you had to begin with irony, born in a place with such a name as that. Life was pepper and salt and nothing too marvelous might be expected from it. Kavanagh, however, had dreams. "I was in my mother's arms clinging with my small hands to the security of her shoulder. I saw into a far mysterious place that I had long associated with Wordsworth's Ode on Immortality. I believed for many years that I had looked back into a world from whence I came. And perhaps I had." As a dreamer he was regarded as something of a fool (hence the title of the book), the butt of jokes at wake, fair, or dance. But, he writes, "being made a fool of is good for the soul. It produces a sensitivity of one kind or another; it makes a man into something unusual, a saint or a poet or an imbecile." He did not blame the people who needed a fool about. There were others who cared for him deeply. An old story: the poet very much of the people, yet set apart from most; nothing, however, of the poet set entirely apart, no Zarathustra nonsense.

"In our house," Kavanagh writes, "the most important subjects were the saying of the Rosary each evening and the making of money. Ours was a united house, there was only one purse let it be full or empty. In other houses the man held to what he could make from cattle or corn, the wife would have to supply the kitchen from the proceeds of butter and eggs. Everybody was poor and proud. My parents didn't know anything to be proud of, so they just carried on." Religion was taken seriously but the priests were judged on their merits as human beings, one regarded as a saint, another as an idiot, with reverence due not them but the function they fulfilled. Throughout his life Kavanagh was neither anti- nor pro-clerical, and he was always Ulster-practical about his relations with the Church. Later, during hard times in Dublin, he would accept quietly small sums of money from the Reverend John McQuaid, the ultra-conservative Archbishop of Dublin.

When Kavanagh was about six years old he went to confession for the first time, not sure why, since his sins were not bothering him much and no one had told him to go. Old Father MacElroy, white-haired and deaf, asked him what sins he remembered, and the child confessed he had committed adultery and stolen from the press.

"Well now, you mustn't steal from the press any more," he advised me tenderly. "And for your penance," he hurriedly summoned up, "for your penance you'll say . . . No, you'll come in and serve my Mass on Sunday."

I take it that young Patrick had no idea what adultery was and that the deaf priest convinced himself he wasn't hearing properly. What comes across, apart from the humor, is matter-of-fact kindliness. Other priests, particularly those who preach hysterically against sex, Kavanagh merely laughs at. They are of no great importance, simply part of the landscape. The nightly Rosary is often a bore, but also a family ritual, like tea or the daily chores. Reading *The Green Fool* one can understand why, if we are to believe certain surveys, most Irish Catholics cease practicing their religion when they emigrate to Birmingham, Manchester, Liverpool, or London. At home Catholicism is worn comfortably and thoughtlessly, but in a different society the faith loses its integral function. The religion is not renounced, only left behind and on lonely evenings remembered regretfully, like family faces.

Except for his dreaming and a fascination with poetry from the age of eight or nine, Kavanagh passed his youth like the rest of the lads, thinning turnips, spraying the potatoes, hauling dung in a cart, and, sporadically, attending the Kednaminsha grade school. He often played truant and quit school forever at the age of twelve. The long summer evenings, when the light would not fail till after ten, were good for mischief. There was the occasional salmon poaching in the River Fane, penny pitching, cards, and more exotic pastimes, catching and killing bees and giving them a wake with pipes and tobacco and whiskey: the deceased were buried like Pharaohs in matchbox coffins under pyramids of dust. To the boy

> It was the garden of the golden apples
> A long garden between a railway and a road. . . .
>
> In the thistly hedge old boots were flying sandals
> By which we travelled through the childhood skies,
> Old buckets rusty-holed with half-hung handles
> Were drums to play when old men married wives.
>
> ("The Long Garden," 1946)

Kavanagh would visit the Carrick Fair, perhaps driving a heifer for sale, and watch bargains being struck in the old manner, a third party bringing the hands of the hagglers together when a fair price had been reached. Once when he was in his early twenties, he sold himself out to hire as a laborer for a Cavan farmer.

> "Were ye ever hired afore?" my man said.
> "No," I answered.
> "Well, before I bid anything, can ye milk?"
> "I can milk anything but a hen," I said.
> "Ha, ha, ha," they laughed, but only like men to whom laughter caused pain.

The arrangement did not last long. The farmer kept getting him up earlier and earlier, the food got worse and worse, and to his relief Kavanagh managed to get himself fired, after breaking a plough.

In 1921 Kavanagh involved himself with the I.R.A., never formally joining but helping out with the pulling down of telegraph wires. His sympathies were Republican (this was the Civil War period) but he thought of his activities more as pranks than as serious military maneuvers. Three of his crowd, however, were caught, lined up against the Dundalk jail wall and shot by the Free Staters. Kavanagh was purged of any simple-minded sort of patriotism or anti-British feeling by the spectacle of Irishmen slaughtering each other, and he came to regard his own limited participation with an amused contempt.

After his failure as a hired hand, his father apprenticed him to the shoemaker's trade, but he was bored by it, so the family managed to purchase an extra three acres of land, his watery hills, he would later call them. He farmed them, but it was only at poetry that he worked hard, from early on: "Around twelve or so I took to the poeming, as it is called. Quite a lot of terror filled the hearts of my parents when they heard the news. 'Was he going to be another Bard?'" There was a local bard, a cripple with an ass and cart and a crockery business, who called himself the Bard of Callenberg. Kavanagh gives the right comic touch to his description of this vestige of the *fili*, druidic poets of pre-Christian Ireland, known especially for their satire, which had the power to kill. Once, after Kavanagh had begun to publish verses in the Poet's Corner of the *Weekly Independent* and in the *Dundalk Democrat*, an agitated man called on him: "Ye can do a great deal for me ... I'm an unfortunate man livin' among the worst of bad neighbors; night, noon and mornin' they have me persecuted. I want ye to make a ballad on them, a good, strong, poisonous ballad. . . . I'll give ye the facts, and you'll make the ballad." He gave the names of his neighbors and their nicknames, which of them had bastard blood and which had been accused of theft, a crime more digraceful than murder in Ireland. It looked to be "the bones of a good ballad." But Ka-

vanagh asked three pounds for it, and the man had only
the price of a couple of bottles of porter. He left, saying
he could get a solicitor cheaper. Aside from its comicality
the incident illustrates Kavanagh's Ulster hard-headed-
ness and foreshadows his later devotion to satirical
verse, which if it had not the power to kill, could wound.

The earliest influences on Kavanagh's poetry were
romantic, the lyrics of Thomas Moore and James
Clarence Mangan, which he found in school texts. They
spoke to his imagination of what was fantastic and unreal
and they fed his dreams. Over the years his technique
advanced and his perceptions widened and sharpened.
It was his imaginative sense or longing and not any active
disgust with Inniskeen that caused him to walk like a
pilgrim to Dublin in 1930. He had been reading William
Carleton, the author of *Traits and Stories of the Irish
Peasantry* (1830–33), who, as he tells in his *Life*, made a
similar journey on foot as a poor scholar, and one can be
sure that Kavanagh had Carleton as a hero in his head as
he made his way south through Slane, begging successfully in some places and getting doors slammed in his face
at others, inquiring at last at the National Library of
Gogarty's address and supposedly having his mis-
fortunate encounter with Gogarty's maid. George Russell (AE), who had played an important role in the
Literary Renaissance both as a writer and as an encour-
ager of young talent, had already printed three of Kavanagh's poems in the *Irish Statesman,* and when
Kavanagh called on him, luck changed. Russell loaded
Kavanagh up with books—Emerson, Melville, Dostoev-
sky, Whitman, James Stephens, Liam O'Flaherty,
Frank O'Connor and others—and with kindness. From
that point on Kavanagh's sights were set on Dublin,

though he did not move there permanently until 1939.

His mixed emotions about finally departing Inniskeen are crystallized in *Tarry Flynn*, completed in 1947, published the next year, and reprinted twice since. The novel was adapted for the stage by P.J. O'Connor and Pat Layde; it had a successful run at the Abbey in 1966 and has been revived frequently since at various theaters around the country. The stage version confines itself mainly to the humorous episodes of the book, the feuds between families, the sharp speech of the mother ("What in the name of the devil's father are you looking for at such an hour of the morning? Are you going to go to Mass at all or do you mean to be at home with them atself? . . . Looking on top of the dresser! Mind you don't put the big awkward hooves on one of them chickens that's under you."), the elaborate attempts to marry-off daughters, the comical intensities of country religion. A girl is knocked off her bicycle at a crossroads by local louts. This causes the parish priest to work himself into a fit over the plague of lust that he sees devastating the townland: "Rapscallions of hell," he preaches, "curmudgeons of the devil that are less civilised than the natives of the Congo. Like a lot of pigs that you were after throwing cayenne pepper among . . . ." He brings in the Redemptorist fathers, famous for their puritanical strictures, for a mission against sex. Of course there is hardly any sex at all going on in the place, but the Redemptorists have the effect of firing everyone up.

A wonderful episode, and typical of *Tarry Flynn*. It covers much of the same ground as *The Green Fool,* but Kavanagh's experience with the law of libel induced him to protect himself with fiction, so the names are changed to protect the innocent author, and the setting is nomi-

nally County Cavan. Aesthetically it is superior to the
earlier work, more humorous, tighter, and more coherent
by virtue of its controlling theme, the inevitable de-
parture from the countryside of its young poet-hero
Tarry.

The time span of the book is confined to Kavanagh's
(or Tarry's) late twenties, that prolonged adolescence
that is the burden and the pleasure of Irish youth. Kavanagh's father, with whom he had been very close, had
died in 1929, and so in the novel the mother is head of the
household, immensely strong, with a curl to her tongue,
but as for Tarry, "she loved that son more than any
mother ever loved a son. She hardly knew why. There was
something so natural about him, so real and so innocent
and which yet looked like badness." He does his work
about the place, but he dreams and reads in the fields,
and at night he scribbles away at verse. He loves a girl but
is too shy to declare it. He loves his district but in his
fantasy-ridden mind he dwells elsewhere, somewhere,
nowhere. Finally an uncle visits and urges Tarry to leave
with him. There'll be a job and money to spend. "It's not
what you make but what you spend that makes you rich."
Abruptly, Tarry decides to go. He appears for breakfast
in his good suit, and the mother knows. Her lips move,
but there are no words. "Then a storm of sobs swept over
her and words came in a deluge. 'Your nice wee place;
your strong farm; your wee room for your writing, your
room for your writing.'"

Kavanagh leaves us at last with the pain of uprooting
and the beauty of what Tarry loves. No bitterness, no
resentment at the stony grey soil, only sadness and confusion at the power of home and the urge to leave it.
Kavanagh had gone away with a book already pub-

lished, another published though aborted, and literary prospects and contacts established in Dublin. Tarry has none of these, but his regret is Kavanagh's own. He had to leave to try himself in the world, but lest we be in any doubt of the price, he ends the novel with a poem and these lines: "And then I came to the haggard gate,/And I knew as I entered that I had come/Through fields that were part of no earthly estate."

3

Adventures in the Bohemian Jungle

For several years Kavanagh shared flats in Dublin with his brother, Peter, who taught at a Christian Brothers school in Westland Row while completing his Ph.D. dissertation, a history of the Abbey Theater, at Trinity College. Peter was his brother's disciple, and later he would become his evangelist. Between Peter's small salary and the steady articles and book and film reviews Patrick did for the *Irish Times*, the *Irish Independent*, the *Irish Press*, and the *Standard*, they made a bare go of it. (Patrick did about 225 pieces for the *Standard* alone, between 1942 and 1949.) Meanwhile he kept on with his verse and became an active giver and receiver of what Yeats called "The daily spite of this unmannerly town."

In those days the Palace Bar in Fleet Street was the center of literary activity or at least talk. R.M. Smyllie, editor of the *Irish Times*, a principal source of employment for writers, presided. Here Kavanagh's satirical verse was spawned. In a discarded fragment of a novel he described the scene:

> He called into the pub where the poets who did not write met on Monday and Thursday evenings. There they were

all of them sitting praising each other and talking literature all the time. 'That line had what Belloc calls the unwanted spondee' he heard one small particularly stupid versifier say. Although he had written much verse in his time Michael did not rightly know what a spondee was. The last time he had seen the word was in a textbook for the Intermediate Examination. . . .

The conversation at the tables was usually drivel. There were no standards of criticism. That destructive element of inarticulate Dublin society which became articulate in Gogarty and James Joyce was here represented. A poisonous element, bitter, clever, good at making hateful witticisms about their neighbors. But they had nothing creative to their name. . . .

At first Kavanagh concealed in verse if not in speech his contempt for this and related Dublin scenes, turning instead against Monaghan as a way of trying to shake the clay from his boots. But he was never absorbed into this society, though he became important to it as a character, a tolerated scourge. He acquired a reputation as a wild and eccentric poet, mostly because of his bluntness—"I don't know you and I don't want to know you"—and the aggressive, controversial nature of his reviews, which attacked the general level of taste in the country. It was a way of calling attention to himself, and it worked, not entirely to his advantage, because it enabled people to pigeonhole him as an oddity, a green fool. But the poet had to eat. Archbishop McQuaid, as mentioned above, occasionally gave him small gifts of money, but when Kavanagh asked him to help him get a job, His Excellency's best effort was to persuade a Dublin bed manufacturer to offer Kavanagh £2/15 a week for carrying planks. Kavanagh declined.

He became known and he knew people, but it was

lonely. In a way he occupied the outsider's place in Dublin that he had in Inniskeen, but without home comforts and land comforts. His anger at the city broke into verse:

> Through the jungle of Pembroke Road
> I have dragged myself in terror
> Listening to the lions of Frustration roar,
> The anguish of beasts that have had their dinner
> And found there was something inside
> Gnawing away unsatisfied.
>
> ("The Jungle," 1948)

This jungle is the Ballsbridge district, prosperous and respectable, where Kavanagh lived out most of his Dublin years. Dwelling among the well-off accentuated his distress. He yearned for success, though he could not respect those who had achieved it this way or that. Often he spoke of marrying a rich woman as the only way a poet could live decently. He had haunts where he made snug, Parson's Bookshop at Baggott Street Bridge for morning tea, the banks of the Grand Canal for sun and meditation, but he was a wanderer. The children knew him and would call out "Paddy! Paddy!" at his approach. His chief pubs were farther into the heart of the city off Grafton Street, McDaid's and the Bailey; as the years advanced he spent more time in them.

The hate runs on uncontrolled in "The Jungle," but in other poems Kavanagh leashes hate to irony and the satiric knife cuts deeper, cleaner:

> Outside this pig-sty life deteriorates,
> Civilisation dwindles. We are the last preserve
> Of Eden in a world of savage states.
> With a touch more cunning and a touch more nerve

You'd establish at the trough your own good place;
Meet all the finest sows if you would just
Not damn each hog you meet straight to his face;
They're all your friends if you but knew. Please put
Your skyward turned snout unto the ground
And nuts that Africa never knew you'll find.

("The Defeated," 1951)

In the plain, conversational style of which he was becoming a master, Kavanagh catches the envious defensiveness of the provincial capital and implies his place in it. His satire has this in common with his lyrical verse, that it requires no formal exegesis, only an ear. To damn each hog or praise each violet straight to its face was his way.

To him the Dublin writers were most of them frauds and bores trying to capitalize on "the Irish thing" and doing their best to diminish and exclude the genuine article, Kavanagh. "The Paddiad" (1949), inspired by Pope's "Dunciad," makes fatuous the writers of Catholic novels, pious verse, Tourist Board pap disguised as poetry:

In the corner of a Dublin pub
This party opens—blub-a-blub—
Paddy Whiskey, Rum and Gin
Paddy Three Sheets on the wind;
Paddy of the Celtic Mist,
Paddy Connemara West,
Chestertonian Paddy Frog
Croaking nightly in the bog.
All the Paddies having fun
Since Yeats handed in his gun. . . .

Celtic Mist, Connemara West, and Frog are based on three writers Kavanagh held in especially low regard: Austin Clarke (a generally admired and prolific poet), Roibeard O'Farachain (novelist and poet), and M.J. McManus (literary editor of the *Irish Press*). Or so Kavanagh named them in a letter to his brother, but they are recognizable types and could represent any number of people. "The Paddiad" mocks the backscratching, self-perpetuating apparatus of Irish letters. The devil appears as patron of the Paddies, offering a bounty for the best poet in each of the 32 counties: "How many poems, Mist, can you spare/For my new anthology of Clare?"

Into the pub steps Paddy Conscience, an amalgam of Stephen Dedalus, the satirical Yeats, Sean O'Casey, and Kavanagh, who tears, raves, uses bad language, and gets thrown out for disturbing cheerful, complacent decorum. News arrives that another embodiment of Paddy Conscience has died in Paris. The Paddies despised and feared Joyce when he was alive; now they honor him "Our wives will make a green silk shroud/To weave him in. The Emerald Isle/Must bury him in tourist style." A broadcast will be held, a monument dedicated.

In "Adventures in the Bohemian Jungle," a verse play first published in John Ryan's *Envoy* magazine in 1950, Kavanagh takes on the entire Dublin art world, literature, theater, painting, music, all tightly bound to commerce. The scene combines the nighttown episode of *Ulysses*, the *Inferno*, and *Pilgrim's Progress*. Kavanagh appears as the simple Countryman, full of love, believer in the power of poets, bewildered by this temple of the Muses, which is nothing more than a drunken party. Count O'Mulligan arrives in a large car. He is the wealthy father of Sheila O'Mulligan, star of "Cardinal Error," and he "brings with him two gross of gold, diamond-studded replicas of the Ardagh Chalice as Cups to be competed for at the Drama Festival." Father John, Chaplain of the Catholic Cultural League, offers two gross of rosary beads to the performers. Politicians carry flags, an American complains that Necessity Number One is not obviously available. "*American*: If there's no Sex, what good is my shillelagh?/*Travelman*: The situation is improving daily." A Guide leads the Countryman through the maze of patrons, sycophants, boozey women. He vomits. He is introduced to Count O'Mulligan but will not speak to him.

> I know him;
> He once employed a poet at his factory
> At thirty bob a week
> And gave ten thousand pounds to the C.C.L.
> He has never committed rape or bigamy it is true
> Goes to Mass every morning in fact
> A good beginning to the businessman's day. . . .
> A charitable man is Count O'Mulligan
> Chairman of the Christian Beggars' Guild
> Benign, bountiful—evil.

Newspapermen interview Sheila O'Mulligan on such subjects as the atomic bomb, television wages, America's outstanding mind, whether the Irish are still the spiritual leaders of mankind, whether religion is still the force in Filmland.

The Countryman had dreamed of sin as fire, "A Maytime-in-the-fields desire," but here he sees but "Tepid fevers, nothing hot,/None alive enough to rot," all secondhand and boring, and he wants out. The poem ends as he joins a urinating contest, wins, "but is later arrested and charged with committing a public nuisance."

Kavanagh wrote many poems in this vein, often appearing himself in the role of *naïf* or indignant truth-teller. They were worthy efforts, slashingly funny, but one can keep at such stuff only so long. It is the sort of satire that has behind it a reforming urge, a messianic impulse, and when poem after poem would appear in newspaper or little magazine, raise a few titters, cause people to say the equivalent of "Kavanagh's done it again, what a droll fellow, I understand he is unkempt and drinks to excess, clever writer though, a genius, surely, or near-genius," and disappear down the rat hole of notoriety—when this would happen again and again, Kavanagh felt wasted, empty, a failure. And often, when he was not writing satire, he would write about failure:

> I never lived, I have no history,
> I deserted no wife to take another,
> I rotted in a room and leave—this message.
>
> The morning newspapers and the radio
> Announced his death in a few horrid words:
> —A man of talent who lacked the little more
> That makes the difference
> Between success and failure.
>   ("Portrait of the Artist," 1951)

The poem expresses contempt for popular standards of success but also Kavanagh's cold misery at feeling unrecognized. Futility, neglect, frustration, he knew them, however well he understood the inadequacy of journalistic judgments. After twelve years in Dublin and more than twice as many years writing poetry, after hundreds of articles and reviews, his rent was in arrears. He was still obliged to keep an eye out for the odd quid, a talk for the B.B.C., an advance for a book he never wrote on

Irish pilgrimages. His brother, Peter, now teaching at an American university, helped all he could, but it was not that Patrick was starving, more that the ceaseless worry about money and the lack of tangible literary fame often wore down his spirit, though he was always full of projects and never despairing. Isolated insults and rebuffs irritated too. In 1951 the Irish Cultural Committee agreed to pay his fare round-trip to America for a tour of readings and lectures, but the Minister for External Affairs, Mr. Frank Aiken, vetoed the Committee's offer. Was Kavanagh subversive of Irish-American relations? Fianna Fail, Eamon De Valera's governing political party, seemed to think so. "I always knew instinctively," Patrick wrote Peter, "that Fianna Fail was the dirtiest, lowest crowd we ever had. I didn't vote for the bastards. . . . I am not really over-worried over Aiken's act and am looking forward to making him look like what he is and all the crowd—loutish enemies etc."

On Saturday, April 12, 1952, Patrick and Peter launched the revenge-vehicle, *Kavanagh's Weekly, A Journal of Literature and Politics.* Peter had saved $3,000 from his professorship, and he returned to Dublin to give financial backing, his knowledge of the mechanics of printing and distributing a newspaper, and to contribute articles. Patrick wrote all the editorials, random social comments, theater, art, book and film reviews, children's stories, and poems. A very few additional articles were written by others, including Myles na gCopaleen (Flann O'Brien). The paper ran to eight pages, or about 10,000 words, per week, sold for sixpence, and averaged well under one tiny advertisement each issue. It lasted thirteen weeks. The brothers got no outside support and stopped when Peter's money ran out.

The history of twentieth-century literature is of course filled with little papers and magazines that, though short lived, make their mark. The student of modern Irish literature and society can look to *Kavanagh's Weekly* as a superb source of social comment on the Ireland of the 1950s. Unfortunately it can be read now only in a handful of private collections, but perhaps someday someone will have wit and means enough to reprint it. A few typical samples will suggest the quality of its observations and tone:

On the theater:

> The Group Theatre is long established and in its early days staged the right kind of plays, some good, some bad, by Ibsen, J.J. Bernard, Odets and Shaw. Then something or someone went wrong and we have had an incessant run of George Shields, St. John Ervine and other grim locals, all presenting lying and hedonistic portraits or rural and urban Ulster, assisted by actors ineluctably bent on ignoring the true, subtle accents of these environments, preferring facile mimicry and cheapest caricature for the laughs they receive from the baboons who are their constant audience.

On politics:

> Among the many charges brought against the Communist philosophy is the one that the individual is of no importance in the Communist state. To which we might answer: is the individual of any importance in any of the Western democratic states?
>
> In Ireland, for instance, a man if he is an individualist, is not imprisoned, he is starved into silence. If the Soviet State sends the non-party-liner to Siberia, ours sends him to Birmingham.

On literature:

> Somerville and Ross were Protestants—in theory at any

rate—but they evoked something valid in Irish life by their pantheism. The ditches and lanes come alive in Somerville and Ross. There is nothing as valid as that in Synge.

His peasants are picturesque conventions; the language he invented for them did a disservice to letters in this country by drawing our attention away from the common speech whose delightfulness comes from its very ordinariness. One phrase of Joyce is worth all Synge as far as giving us the cadence of Irish speech. . . .

Since writing all this I have re-read 'The Playboy' and I find—that Synge has imposed on the peasant women . . . a psychology which is only to be found among the higher types of women. It is only the sophisticated, educated woman who has the courage to worship the hero. . . . Synge found Pegeen Mike among the sophisticated upper class women of Paris or Dublin and put her in an incongruous setting. From this point of view he flattered the peasants.

These excerpts give the general tone of *Kavanagh's Weekly,* one of ridicule with a reforming impulse behind it. Myles na gCopaleen's contributions, while typically brilliant, are inconsistent with the rest of the paper because of the nihilistic premise of their humor. For Kavanagh the political, literary and everyday follies of Ireland were targets of fun, but he imagined that his criticism might enlighten, might reduce the number of asses. Partly because of the failure of his paper, he gave up such hopes eventually.

Their money gone and with no prospects of outside assistance, the Kavanaghs burned all but 100 of the last edition of the *Weekly*, No. 13, and managed to sell thirteen of these at £5 each. Bitterly and not a little petulantly Patrick wrote in his final editorial:

We would go so far as to say that not only has Irish society never believed in the value of literature but it has never believed in Christianity. There is no dramatic abandon in

Irish society, no wild enthusiasm for any special idea as in
England.

   ... Ireland ... established to its own satisfaction its
poetic and saintly nature while at the same time attributing
to the English who have produced what is probably the
greatest literature of mankind the qualities of stolidity, un-
imaginativeness, lack of poetic life.

   This is a very curious affair and it may have something to
do with 'compensations' of a Freudian kind.

Having attacked practically everyone of any political,
literary, or social note individually, he ended by damn-
ing the entire Irish nation and committing the sin
against the Holy Ghost, praising England by contrast.

   Inevitably attempts were made to get back at Kavanagh for the *Weekly* and for his attacks in other publica-
tions. Already in April, 1948, an anonymous article in
The Bell had referred to him as "a stage Irishman about
town," had said that he "shares with Mr. Frank Sinatra,
Dylan Thomas, Picasso and the Marx Brothers the
capacity for arousing the emotions to the screaming
point for or against him," and that, with reference to his
teeth, "it would be a poor vet who could not tell Mr.
Kavanagh's age from them." Kavanagh occasionally
complained to editors about such stuff but for the most
part ignored it. When three months after the closing of
the *Weekly* a "Profile" of him appeared in *The Leader*,
however, Kavanagh sued. The article portrayed him

   hunkering on a bar-stool, defining alcohol as the worst
   enemy of the Imagination. ... With a malevolent insult
   which, naturally, is well received, the Master orders a
   further measure, and, cocking an eye at the pub-clock,
   downs the malt in a gulp which produces a fit of coughing
   which all but stops the traffic outside. His acolytes—sylph-
   like redheads, dewy-eyed brunettes, two hard-faced intel-

lectual blondes, three rangy university poets and several semi-bearded painters—flap: 'Yous have no merit, no merit at all'—he insults them individually and collectively, they love it, he suddenly leaves to get lunch in the Bailey and have something to win on the second favourite. He'll be back.

The general impression given of Kavanagh is of an alcoholic sponger and self-praiser, with a rare poetic talent hidden beneath a "labyrinthian jungle" of foolish and useless opinions on subjects he knows nothing about. In his claim, Kavanagh stated that the "Profile" had gravely damaged his reputation and profession, causing odium, hatred, ridicule and contempt to be heaped upon him.

How much Kavanagh believed in his own claim it is difficult to say. Certainly he thought there was a good chance a jury would believe it. The case came to trial on February 4, 1954. The High Court filled with spectators, crowds formed outside. The *Irish Times* gave extensive coverage, reprinted in Kavanagh's *Collected Pruse* (1967), and today there are people in Dublin who cherish copies of the complete transcript. Not the least reason for all this interest is that the chief counsel for the defendants, Mr. John A. Costello, had been Taoiseach (Prime Minister of the Republic) from 1948–51 and would become Taoiseach again soon after the trial from 1954–57. For thirteen hours spread over four days Mr. Costello hammered at Kavanagh in the witness box, trying to prove, as his chief lines of defense for *The Leader*, these arguments: that Kavanagh had said in print things about other writers and political figures as bad or worse than anything said about him in *The Leader*; that portions of Kavanagh's works had been banned for indecency; that articles just as critical or more so about the plaintiff had been appearing for years, yet plaintiff had taken no action on them; that, in spite of its criticism, the article praised Kavanagh as Ireland's greatest living poet; and that, far from damaging his reputation and profession, the article had actually increased Kavanagh's fame and thereby his income. In addition, Mr. Costello's strategy was to exhaust Kavanagh with extended interrogation, hoping the pressure would break the poet's nerve.

Kavanagh did not break although, aware of Mr. Costello's strategy, he pretended to collapse on the last day of questioning (or so his brother states), heightening the impression that he was being persecuted. The testimony reveals Kavanagh's shrewdness and toughness, and his ripostes repeatedly caused laughter in the courtroom and make extremely amusing reading. When Mr. Costello asked whether he had implied that Austin Clarke was not a sufficiently good poet to be employed on the radio, Kavanagh replied, "I will answer without 'yes' or 'no.' What would the doctors say about a quack who was given a job in Vincent's Hospital?" Thus he managed to avoid answering the question and to avoid defaming someone directly in court. Asked if he had not himself written about his spending time and money in pubs, Kavanagh said that it was imaginative writing and had nothing to do with reality: "You might as well take Agatha Christie, who writes murder stories, and accuse her of the murder in one of her books." Questioned about passages in *Kavanagh's Weekly*, he took advantage of having written many of his pieces under pseudonyms, denied having written them, attributed them to his brother, or said that many things were added "by others" just to fill out column inches. (These must not have been the most convincing of his evasions.)

The trial was a sparring match. Mr. Costello won over the jury. From the legal point of view, Mr. Costello built a good defense, but in his responses Kavanagh was as clever as Bertolt Brecht before the United States House of Representatives Un-American Activities Committee, and much funnier. The adversaries gained respect for one another. At one point, Mr. Costello asked whether it wasn't true that there were a vast number of people who did not agree with Kavanagh's point of view. "There is," Kavanagh answered sharply, "a small, pernicious minority which you represent." Then he paused, a little startled by himself. "Is that wrong?" he asked. "I am sorry to say that. I am very sorry."

"Ah, Mr. Kavanagh," said Mr. Costello, "I don't mind."

It is a revealing moment, the gloves dropped briefly. And it foreshadows a great irony. In May, 1955, when Mr. Costello again held the office of Taoiseach, he arranged through private negotiations, at his own initiative, for Kavanagh to receive from University College, Dublin, an annual stipend for life of £400. The previous Christmas Kavanagh had sent Mr. Costello a portion of a poem:

> Note well the face profoundly grave,
> An empty mind can house a knave.
> Be careful to show no defiance,
> They've made pretence into a science;
> Card-sharpers of the art committee
> Working all the provincial cities,
> They cry 'Eccentric' if they hear
> A voice that seems at all sincere.

Fold up their table and their gear
And with the money disappear.

The Taoiseach had replied with a Christmas card and a note:

Dear Patrick Kavanagh,
   I wish I could acknowledge more gracefully and more substantially the grace and substance of "From a Prelude."
Thank you very much.

4

Freedom

Take me to the top of the high hill
Mount Olympus laughter-roaring unsolemn
Where no one is angry and satirical
About a mortal creature on a tall column.
("Freedom," 1958)

Kavanagh's progress, if that is the right word, reminds me of Samuel Beckett's many-named hero, Murphy-Watt-Molloy-Moran-Malone-Unnamable, who after years of searching, cursing, hating, wondering, wandering, loses his last possessions, confronts death, casts off his selves and self-fictions and gives himself up to pure contemplation of the space around him; Kavanagh wifeless, curling up sometimes in basements, sloping about Dublin "dishevelled with shoes untied," taken as one thing by onlookers while a contradictory poetic universe whirled in his head, confronts death and achieves for a moment equilibrium in poetry that contemplates whatever corner he finds himself occupying. Of course the analogy is imperfect: it was during the last years that he had his University stipend and, seven months before his death, he married. But he thought *Waiting for Godot* a great play because it "put despair and futility on the stage for us to laugh at. . . . Beckett is an honest writer. Academic writers and painters are always ready to offer the large illuminating symbol; they give us gods and heroes, and they write and paint as if society were a solid, unified Victorian lie."

On March 31, 1955, Kavanagh was operated on for cancer of the lung. The lung was removed. Unaccountably he recovered completely, was out of the hospital in three weeks and convalesced at the Royal Hibernian Hotel, one of Dublin's most luxurious, with Peter footing the bill. Some disappointment greeted his return to relative health, as he was to have been waked in the City Hall. Always humor in any of Kavanagh's exploits, even almost dying—but barely eluding death had a serious and positive effect on his poetry. It was after this that he wrote three or four of his finest lyrics, permanent ones, I think, that will with *The Great Hunger* make his monument. Kavanagh himself thought that he had not become a poet until after his illness, and while the judgment is too narrow, it has its truth. His sickness deprived him of a lung and of much hatred, or let us say that the trauma of his cancer made the targets of his hatred seem as petty as they were and as unworthy of his continuous attention. In "The Hospital" (1956) he wrote of love:

> A year ago I fell in love with the functional ward/Of a chest hospital: square cubicles in a row/Plain concrete, wash basins—an art lover's woe,/Not counting how the fellow in the next bed snored./But nothing whatever is by love debarred./The common and banal her heat can know./The corridor led to a stairway and below/Was the inexhaustible adventure of a gravelled yard.

Simple, original, moving; a return to the naming and praising of his early verse but without gush or awe-struck pose; the language common as the subject. Kavanagh's love is that of distinterested (selfless, if you like) appreciation. It was that way with women, too, for at least from the evidence of his poems his love was rarely requited. Love is pursued, missed, remembered: "On Raglan Road on an autumn day I met her first and knew/That her dark hair would weave a snare that I might one day rue;/ I saw the danger, yet I walked along the enchanted way,/And I said, let grief be a fallen leaf at the dawning of the day. . . . " Written to the meter of the Irish air, "The Dawning of the Day," in 1946, "On Raglan Road" is typical of Kavanagh's love poetry in theme even if he varied his language and form over the years. By 1958 the style has been carved down to the bare bones but love remains a thing of memory, a lost chance:

> She waved her body in the circle sign
> Of love purely born without side;
> The earth's contour, she orbited to my pride,
> Sin and unsin.
> But the critic asking questions ran
> From the fright of the dawn
> To weep later on an urban lawn
> For the undone
> God-gifted man.
> ("Love in a Meadow")

But if women, like fame, eluded him, he felt after his illness that he was free to love without bitterness those things of which he asked nothing but their existence: the natural world, man-made objects acted on by nature and by time, even women when they were out of reach in memory or fancy:

No, no, no, I know I was not important as I moved
Through the colourful country, I was but a single
Item in the picture, the namer not the beloved.
O tedious man with whom no gods commingle.
Beauty, who has described beauty? Once upon a time
I had a myth that was a lie but it served:
Trees walking across the crests of hills and my rhyme
Cavorting on mile-high stilts and the unnerved
Crowds looking up with terror in their rational faces.
O dance with Kitty Stobling I outrageously
Cried out-of-sense to them, while their timorous paces
Stumbled behind Jove's page boy paging me.
I had a very pleasant journey, thank you sincerely
For giving me my madness back, or nearly.

> ("Come Dance with Kitty Stobling," 1958)

Poetry had become all. As in "The Hospital," naming is the love-act. Poetry is not one activity in life, it is life itself, the lover's means of seeing and feeling, letting the gods commingle, out-of-sense, unreasonable.

"That a poet is born, not made, is well known," Kavanagh said in 1963 in a "Self-Portrait" broadcast over Irish television.

> But this does not mean that he was a poet the day he was physically born. For many a good-looking year I wrought at versing but I would say that, as a poet, I was born in or about nineteen-fifty-five, the place of my birth being the banks of the Grand Canal.
>
> Thirty years earlier Shancoduff's watery hills could have done the trick, but I was too thick to take the hint. Curious this, how I had started off with the right simplicity, indifferent to crude reason and then ploughed my way through complexities and anger, hatred and ill-will towards the faults of man, and came back to where I had started.

Kavanagh felt that in order to achieve this right kind

of simplicity, the simplicity of return, he had had to reach a position of what he called "not caring." By this he did not mean cynicism but acceptance of his or any other man's humble place in the world, which would spin regardless of him but which was worth observing and capturing in words, whatever the effect, whatever the consequence, the likelihood being that there would be none. Not caring, "we don't care whether we appear foolish or not. We talk of things that earlier would embarrass. We are satisfied with being ourselves, however small. So it was that on the banks of the Grand Canal between Baggot and Leeson Street bridges in the warm summer of 1955, I lay and watched the green waters of the canal. I had just come out of hospital." Three years later he was able to write of "Leafy-with-love banks and the green waters of the canal/Pouring redemption for me, that I do/The will of God, wallow in the habitual, the banal, ... ("Canal Bank Walk," 1958)" This was the first of several canal bank poems celebrating the grass and water running across the south side of Dublin. Children swim in it, boys fish it, office workers take their lunch/beside it, lovers and old people sit along it through afternoons. Roads cross it and run along either side of it, so you cannot forget the city or its busy striving, but the canal is, though man-made, something tranquil and natural in the midst of artifice. It helped Kavanagh recapture himself and helped him not to care. The greatest of his canal bank poems is "Lines Written on a Seat on the Grand Canal, Dublin, 'Erected to the Memory of Mrs. Dermot O'Brien'" (1958):

> O commemorate me where there is water,
> Canal water preferably, so stilly

Greeny at the heart of summer. Brother
Commemorate me thus beautifully.
Where by a lock Niagarously roars
The falls for those who sit in the tremendous silence
Of mid-July. No one will speak in prose
Who finds his way to these Parnassian islands.
A swan goes by head low with many apologies,
Fantastic light looks through the eyes of bridges—
And look! a barge comes bringing from Athy
And other far-flung towns mythologies.
O commemorate me with no hero-courageous
Tomb—just a canal-bank seat for the passer-by.

Kavanagh got rid of a great deal in order to accomplish this sonnet: self-righteousness, self-pity, the temptation to take himself rather than life seriously. He had always insisted on realism, scorning writers who falsified life, but here, as he commented in 1959, he brought about "the final fusion of all crudeness into a pure flame." It is a religious conception of poetry, the poet as priest, language the transubstantiating power. The poem seems borne on the ambient air it describes. Its technique, while unobtrusive, has much to do with its success and is made possible by the new self-confidence that somehow came to Kavanagh after fifty years of age. The rhyme, for example (ababcdcdefgefg), is audacious: "water" with "Brother" (perhaps a slightly Irish "wather" can be heard here); "preferably, so stilly" slides into "thus beautifully"; "roars" with "prose"; "silence" with "islands"; and boldest of all, "bridges" with "courageous." The effect is to make the poem's intensity seem off hand, bottled-up but escaping with graceful pressure, a backhanded catch, the favorite winning by an easy neck.

Writing about ecstasy has its perils. Joyce's cele-
brated epiphany, the beach scene in *A Portrait of the
Artist as a Young Man*, tastes like trifle today, though it
is possible Joyce intended it as an example of how not to
describe visionary experience. The later Yeats provided
Kavanagh with a better model in "Vacillation" where
the dull, off-hand phrase "twenty minutes more or less"
makes the ecstasy of "my body of a sudden blazed"
believable and affecting. Getting the mood into words, it
was essential to convey a mundane setting in colloquial
language—Yeats's shop, cup, and table-top, Kavanagh's
banal canal-bank seat.

"The mark of the poet is his lightness, the pure per-
sonality revealed bare in all its volatility and with the
gaiety that is of God. . . ." So Kavanagh said lecturing
at University College, Dublin, in 1956. He quoted St.
Augustine: "I am conscious of something within me that
plays before my soul and is as a light dancing in front of
me. Were this brought to steadiness and perfection in me
it would surely be eternal light." The mystical impulse
had been with him from the start but not until 1956, and
with greatest effect in 1958, was he able to "record love's
mystery without claptrap" not here and there in an
isolated verse but with a fair consistency. These later
poems are the sequel to *Tarry Flynn*: the poet departed,
travels the road of hate into the city of love and light. In
poetry, at least, and if it is possible to separate Kavanagh's life from his work, it must be said that work
gave him what life never could. There was too much de-
speration in him for personal happiness. He drank a great
deal too much and suffered collapses, about which he
was always flippant and defiant on recovery: "Some of
my friends stayed faithful but quite a handful/Looked

upon it as the end: I could quite safely be/Dismissed as
a dead loss in the final up toss./He's finished and that's
definitely. ("The Same Again," 1966)"

Although the cancer did not recur, he suffered from
thrombosis of the legs and a weak heart, and heavy
smoking caused constant coughing and hoarseness. By
1966 he had been told that if he did not stop drinking he
would die from alcoholic poisoning. On April 19, 1967,
he married Katharine Moloney in Dublin. On November
30 of that year he died. He was buried at Inniskeen.

There is a word, buckleppin', that Kavanagh invented
to convey all that was offensive and ridiculous to him
about "the Irish thing." The bucklep is an act performed
by a man eager to display his merit and exuberence as a
true Gael. He will be gallivanting (another favorite
Kavanagh term of abuse) along some street in Dublin,
and suddenly he will leap into the air with a shout,
causing his heels to strike hard against his buttock-
cheeks. That is buckleppin'. The bucklep or the buck-
lepper may be found in many areas of Irish life but is
especially notable in literature and may take many
forms: a gratuitous reference to Cuchulain, an affected
quaintness of phrasing, a pious nod toward 1916 and all
that, stage-Irish characterization, the cliché mixture of
melancholy and sentimentality, false bravado such as
showy contempt for the Church, or the reverse, false
piety. Kavanagh termed the spending of a quarter of a
million pounds annually on the Irish Radio and Television Service the National Bucklep: all that for ballad
singing, Irish lessons, quiz programs to flatter the ignorant, deadly poetry broadcasts. It was, he said, a
national commitment to the graveyard. Occasionally he
was guilty of a bucklep himself:

My soul was an old horse
Offered for sale in twenty fairs.
I offered him to the Church—the buyers
Were little men who feared his unusual airs. . . .
                ("Pegasus," 1944)

Thin stuff—"loud, journalistic and untrue," he called it in 1963. In the last stanza the old horse grows wings and the poet rides away. But it is only a lapse from his usual standard, and after 1955 it is difficult to find a dishonest line even in his less than brilliant pieces.

In the 'thirties other Irish poets than Kavanagh tried new tacks but they were quite different from his. Samuel Beckett, writing in *The Bookman* in 1934, stated that "contemporary Irish poets may be divided into antiquarians and others, the former in the majority, the latter kindly noticed by Mr. W.B. Yeats as 'the fish that lie gasping on the shore,' suggesting that they might at least learn to expire with an air." The gasping fish interested Beckett, he was one of them. He proclaimed that the old subjects, the old objects, had disintegrated. His way and that more or less of such poets as Denis Devlin, Brian Coffey, and Thomas MacGreevy, was to make the self the only true subject of art. Turn away from the object, which is false, an illusion; turn inward, explore, question, examine the self all the way to *The Unnamable*; place selves contracting, splitting and not interacting on the stage.

For Beckett this approach has been productive of masterpieces, yet it leads eventually to nowhere, as he admitted after finishing his trilogy. And even Beckett, in *Krapp's Last Tape*, wonders whether after all it is only the moments of palpable joyous contact with the Other that count, even as they disappear and become clouded in memory, preserved sharply, poignantly and somewhat absurdly on magnetic tape. For Kavanagh the moment, "the passionate transitory," was always the true poetic subject. The difficulty was in clearing away the claptrap. Violent rejection was a start but, as we have noted, naysaying such as that of *The Great Hunger* carries with it its own distortions. And one of the difficulties Kavanagh faced was that he loved Ireland, not as an abstraction but as specific hills, faces, and phrases, fiercely. The objective world and the mystery emanating from it moved and attracted him, even as the falsifying of that world repelled him or made him laugh. As for the self, or that old nag the soul, he became free and most eloquent when he ceased caring about it. The mystic tries to lose his self in the Other or the One. Kavanagh had his own modest sort of mysticism, losing himself in the Many, a hedge, a hill, a bridge, people, specified and reformed into a poem: "Today in the street I was astonished/The years had left me so unpunished,/I was in love with women— honest! . . . ("A Summer Morning Walk," 1960)"

Mrs. Harden Rodgers Jay, lecturer in English at Trinity College, Dublin, recently wrote of Kavanagh that he is "considered Ireland's major poet since the death of W.B. Yeats. . . . A contradictory and invigorating character, his influence over the younger generation of Irish poets is inestimable." That could mean that he has had no influence at all, but it does not. All the younger poets, and by that I mean poets ranging in age from the mid-forties down to the twenties, seem to find it necessary to declare whether and if so how much they have been influenced by Kavanagh. All would agree, I think, that he did away with what was left of the Literary

Renaissance and the idea of Ireland as a vague spiritual entity. Some, however, believe that he substituted a boastful, proud ignorance of the past for the romantic and nationalistic view of the past that characterized the Renaissance. Some are unwilling to junk the Irish language and its historical associations as Kavanagh did: he was opposed to the requiring of Irish in the schools, and he felt that if misguided people wished to study the language, they should be free to do so, but it was their own problem. Some have stopped at midpoint, as it were, to worry: they reject romantic nationalism, but they ponder the meaning of Ireland and the talismanic nuances of the names of important men and places: Pearse, Connolly, Parnell, Tone, Swift, Sarsfield, Cuchulain, Maeve; Kilmainham, Kinsale, Aughrim, Boyne, Clontarf. Thomas Kinsella, for example, in "A Country Walk," sees the past as so much debris in a river but cannot leave off pondering it and conjuring it. He devoted years to a translation of *The Tain*, the great Cuchulain epic, and, ironically, his translation reveals *The Tain* as poetry of which Kavanagh would have approved: vigorous, uncluttered, humorous and bawdy. Kinsella is very much in the tradition of Pound, Joyce, and Eliot, finding an idiom at ease with past as with present.

But Kavanagh's example has freed many younger Irish poets to find their own subjects and means of expression untrammeled by any tradition. In the case of the most talented of the younger poets, Seamus Heaney, who is thirty-five at the present writing, Kavanagh's influence has been fundamental. Heaney acknowledges that reading Kavanagh made him think that he might have something to write about himself. Like Kavanagh,

Heaney's background is rural, Ulster and Catholic. Un-
like Kavanagh, he has a university education and until
recently taught at Queen's University, Belfast. In spite
of this he began his poetry where Kavanagh left off,
naming, praising, and scrutinizing the life he knows best.
I trust that it takes nothing away from Seumus Heaney's
immense talent to say of a poem such as "The Early
Purges," that many, though not all, of the poem's qualities derive from the inspiration of Kavanagh. Heaney
wrote it in his early twenties, yet already he had the con-
fidence to make poetry out of the prosaic events he had
seen with his own eyes, dealing with them as they are,
with Ulster hardness and sharpness, resisting any urge
to inflate them by gratuitous reference or literary phrasing, mindful of the poetry in the very ordinariness of
Dan Taggart's speech and his own. In fact Heaney has a
greater interest in words than Kavanagh ever did (the
influence here, if any, is Joycean) and he has delighted in
his more recent work in making a poem turn on an odd
or archaic word or phrase. But at the start he saw the gift
Kavanagh offered and had the sense to take it.

What has not as yet been passed on to a succeeding
generation is Kavanagh's willingness, like Yeats's before
him, to involve himself actively if individually in political
and social issues. Several poets have written occasional
verses in reaction to the situation in Northern Ireland,
but aesthetically these works have been inferior, and they
suggest the degree to which the rhetoric of romantic
nationalism blights Irish poetry when it deals directly
with politics. In Ireland poetry and politics have never
been separate. They are not often separate elsewhere
either, but the Irish, like all dominated people, have for
centuries represented an especially dramatic example of

the interpenetration of politics and poetry, life and art, so much so that it becomes impossible to speak of either realm without including the other. In designating *Kavanagh's Weekly* not a journal of the arts but *A Journal of Literature and Politics*, Kavanagh gave formal recognition to this truth, that when a nation's literature is confused about its national identity, it reflects confusion in the nation as a whole. As Conor Cruise O'Brien has pointed out, when Maude Gonne, playing the title role in Yeats's play, *Cathleen ni Houlihan*, called symbolically for the nation's sons to sacrifice themselves for Mother Ireland, the immediate result was a powerful, shocking effect on the audience, and some members of the audience felt moved to take up arms. In 1916, Constance Markiewicz played Cathleen ni Houlihan in a "real life" situation and received a death sentence. She was spared, many others were not, and at last the playwright, near death himself, wondered,

> Did that play of mine send out
> Certain men the English shot?

The probable answer, says Cruise O'Brien, is "Yes, it did."

Today, after Kavanagh, when romantic nationalism seems to have receded from Ireland's literature, it remains a powerful and destructive force in the country, whether it takes the form of Sinn Fein and the I.R.A. or the complementary form of the more fanatical Unionists, who give voice to their own kind of poetry when they toast King William III: ". . . and whoever denies this toast may be slammed, crammed and jammed into the muzzle of the great gun of Athlone." In this atmosphere men, women, and children on both sides are blown up in the name of a United Ireland or King Billy, and politicians talk of the historical unity of the Irish people or the historical independence of Irish Protestants. Some apt Kavanagh lines:

> They put a wreath upon the dead
> For the dead will wear the cap of any racket,
> The corpse will not put his elbows through his jacket
> Or contradict the words some liar has said.
> The corpse can be fitted out to deceive—
> Fake thoughts, fake love, fake ideal,
> And rogues can sell its guaranteed appeal,
> Guaranteed to work and never come alive. . . .
> ("A Wreath for Tom Moore's Statue," 1944)

Kavanagh's obituary in *The Times* was headed: "Reputation for Eccentricity Said to Have Overshadowed Talents as a Writer." How uneccentric he seems now.

Selected Bibliography

Ploughman and Other Poems. London: Macmillan, 1936.

The Green Fool. London: Michael Joseph, 1938; reissued 1971.

The Great Hunger. Dublin: Cuala Press, 1942; reissued 1971.

A Soul for Sale. London: Macmillan, 1947.

Tarry Flynn. Dublin: Pilot Press, 1948; New York: Devin Adair, 1949; London: New English Library, 1962; London: MacGibbon & Kee, 1965, 1968.

Come Dance with Kitty Stobling. London: Longmans, 1960.

Self Portrait. Dublin: Dolmen Press, 1964.

Collected Poems. London: MacGibbon & Kee, 1964; New York: Devin Adair, 1965, over author's protest of copyright infringement. London: Martin, Brian and O'Keeffe, 1973.

Collected Pruse. London: MacGibbon & Kee, 1967; Martin, Brian and O'Keeffe, 1973.

NOTE:

Kavanagh was close throughout his life to his brother, Dr. Peter Kavanagh, a teacher and scholar, who on his own hand press brought out Patrick's *Recent Poems* in 1958. After the poet's death in 1967, Dr. Kavanagh undertook at his own expense, and on his own press, Peter Kavanagh Hand Press, to provide scholars, biographers, and other interested persons with as complete a record as possible of his brother's literary achievements. The author had co-operated in neither of the MacGibbon and Kee collected editions of the poetry and prose, and much more was left out than put in. Since then Dr. Kavanagh has produced four volumes that have been invaluable to me in the preparation of this book: *Lapped Furrows* (1969), containing correspondence and other documents; *November Haggard* (1971), containing uncollected poetry and prose; *The Complete Poems of Patrick Kavanagh* (1972), an edition of 1,000 copies; and *Garden of the Golden Apples* (1972), a bibliography of primary and secondary sources.